Printed in the United States of America

First Printing, 2020

ISBN 978-1-7355916-2-9

Independently Published with Kindle Direct Publishing

Book Website: CommonSense-IThink.com

To Whom it May Concern

Dear Whom,

Well, it's the same old story...Again and Again. It's been told over and over again, in many different ways.

Network marketing will make you wealthy or keep you poor. It will give you happiness or show you sadness. Make you greedy or prove you can share.

It will give you an education or allow you to stay dumb, naive, ignorant, stupid, ooooor a combination of all 5. This is surely where Common Sense comes into play. As you know, you only do 2 things when using your Common Sense.

Common Sense will tell you what is right or wrong, what's good or bad, or what you should do and what you shouldn't do. But, that don't necessarily mean you are going to do it well, if you only have to do 2 things at a time when using Common Sense, you should think that would make your life easy.

RIGHT? WELL, IT WILL REALLY MAKE YOUR LIFE HARD — VERY HARD. AND, HERE'S THE REASON WHY. HUMANS HAVE THE TENDENCY TO MAKE MANY CHOICES IN THEIR LIVES.

"SUCH IS LIFE!"

IF YOU WANT TO DO BETTER IN LIFE, YOU KNOW, TO IMPROVE YOUR SELF, JUST REMEMBER, THE FIELD OF NETWORK MARKETING WILL ALLOW YOU TO CHOOSE — POSITIVE OR NEGATIVE.

YOU CHOOSE.

SINCERELY,
TOM BURNS

INTRODUCTION

IT'S A
PYRAMID

It's a
Scam

They just want
my money

GLENN D. WOODROME

LIFE

YOU

Here are 3 lines
for you to put your own
negative statements.

1._____
2._____
3._____

Once you have your
list, TEAR it out
of this book and...
BURN IT!!!

HAVE I SHOWN ENOUGH THINGS CALLED "EXCUSES"??

WHEN TRYING TO EXPLAIN NETWORK MARKETING.

6

Rules When Going Through This Book!!

Rule #1: The Initials CS will always stand for *COMMEN SENSE*

Rule #2: The initials N-W-M will always stand for *NETWORK MARKETING.*

Rule #3: You don't have to believe anything in this book. You should believe, but you don't have too.

Rule #4: OH, HELL.....we just make them up as we go.

Common Sense is very easy (simple) to use in Network Marketing Industry. Doing things (stuff) in N-W-M isn't all that complicated. You just need to use easy principles. For example:

The Principle of ONE!!!

Let's take a look at all the different opportunities in N-W-M that are offered in the world. There are hundreds and hundreds of companies throughout the planet that will let you represent them. Their products, their services are huge. And, you don't have to invest "Dilly Wad" (very little money) into your own business. And I do mean your OWN Business. You don't need a storefront, heavy inventories, or even a lot of money to buy into this idea. Note: go see what it takes to have any type of franchise. You can operate your business out of your house.

To do this, you just have to represent ONE N-W-M business.

Here is some more good news – (if, you use your common sense correctly) :

You can make a little money or develop a whole new career; get a little bit of stability and security in your life.

And Why Not?

Here are a few good ideas and reasons for thinking about your own business in N-W-M.....

*** You do not have to create your Business Plan from scratch—it's already done by others.

*** You don't need a college degree or a special training school– super training is always available.

*** You don't have to go down the "trail" by yourself– there are support teams everywhere.

*** You don't have to give up your present type of work – N-W-M is called "side-hustle"– build your OWN business in your spare time (part-time).

*** This business adventure can be your own idea– you don't need approval from NOBODY.

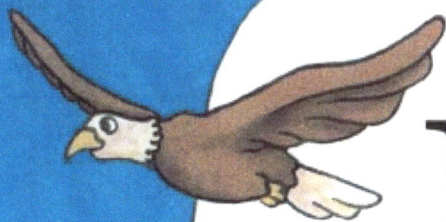

NETWORK MARKETING CAN SAY "HELLO"
IN MANY DIFFERENT LANGUAGES.

Bonjour
Ahoj
Namaste
Hallo
Hej
Bok
HI
Hai
ni hao
Howdy
Dia dhuit
Tere
BULA
HOLA
Hello
Terve
Kon'nichiwa
Hej
Aloha
Salutton
Shalom
Sziasztok
Oi
Ciao
XIN CHÀO
GUTEN TAG

GLENN D. WOODROME

C/S WILL TELL YOU, IN N-W-M

YOU CAN DO THIS ALL THE TIME

WIN

TO DEATH

FROM BIRTH

IF (AND ONLY IF) YOU CONTINUOUSLY IMPROVE YOURSELF!!!

(CLUE: SELF-EDUCATION)

14

RESIDUAL EXPENSES

$ personal Bills · payroll · business Bills · etc · STUDENT LOANS · ? · bills · ? · insurance bills · employee TAXES

RESIDUAL INCOME

Travel VACATIONS The good life

Do you want to guess what most people come up with?

ENTREPENEUR DESIGNERS

ARCHITECT skills Trail blazers Thinkers CHALLENGE

relationships WANDERS Listeners BLOGERS Community ARTISTS opportunity Leaders

DOCTORS neighbors code breakers

NETWORK engineers BUILDERS COMMUNICATE

Family Teachers (WE ARE ALL INVOLVED IN) MARKETING Mentors

Recruiters

planners

OPERATIONS Developer MOTHERS ATTITUDE visionary DREAMERS INNOVATORS Readers BELIEVERS

LAWYERS (MANY PEOPLE DON'T GET PAID FOR IT) STUDENT Passion

FRIENDS SUPPORT intention OPTIMIST Groups

Risk takers Partners Scholars FATHERS Nurses

INDIAN CHIEF Books

videographer

C/S Knows this is the gospel truth

Network Marketing

THE WORLD

YOU

vs

NOT

A SPECTATOR SPORT

10-20-30

1-20-30

You Have to be on the Field to Score

SURF
NETWORK
MARKETING

I DON'T THINK THIS IS WHAT THEY HAD IN MIND. THEY WANT YOU TO DO A LOT OF RESEARCH WORK ON THE **INTERNET** ABOUT NETWORK MARKETING.

CLUE: Don't ever make your decision on what you want out of life, without solid knowledge behind it.

SHRINKING LEISURE TIME

Well, that's a hell of a thing. What are we all working so hard for? Could one of the reasons be---'FREEDOM OF TIME'? Having enough money in life is nice; but, having freedom of time is super nice.

How could someone prepare for the future that gives both money & time? One thing could be called a Residual Income Business. Now, what is Residual Income? Plainly put, it's doing something one time and getting paid for it again and again---month after month. Make your income source work 24/7 for you.

Investments, franchises are good ways to make it happen. Unfortunately, many so-called middle income people don't have the money---up-front money. So what can we do? Here's something that's simple and easy.....NETWORK MARKETING.

SHRINKING LEISURE TIME

Continued....

Please, always remember, to be good @ Network Marketing takes a lot of work on your part---no one else---just you. Thinking about this objection in life can surely keep you up at night.

There are many, many people in the business world who will go through their business life with very little freedom of time. Even when it comes to something called vacations. A tremendous amount of people get vacations. But, they are not 'paid-vacations'. And, even those who get a paid-vacation, the money is so small, when they go on their vacations, they can't even afford getting out of the city limits. Don't you be those type of people--- earn your FREEDOM OF TIME!

In N.W.M, C/S says,

you can go fast,
you can go slow,
but never stop moving ahead!

A rabbit gets somewhere

A snail gets somewhere

TOMORROW

A STRANGE PLACE WHERE 99% OF ALL GREAT THINGS HAPPEN ...OR... WHERE 99% OF ALL BAD THINGS HAPPEN.

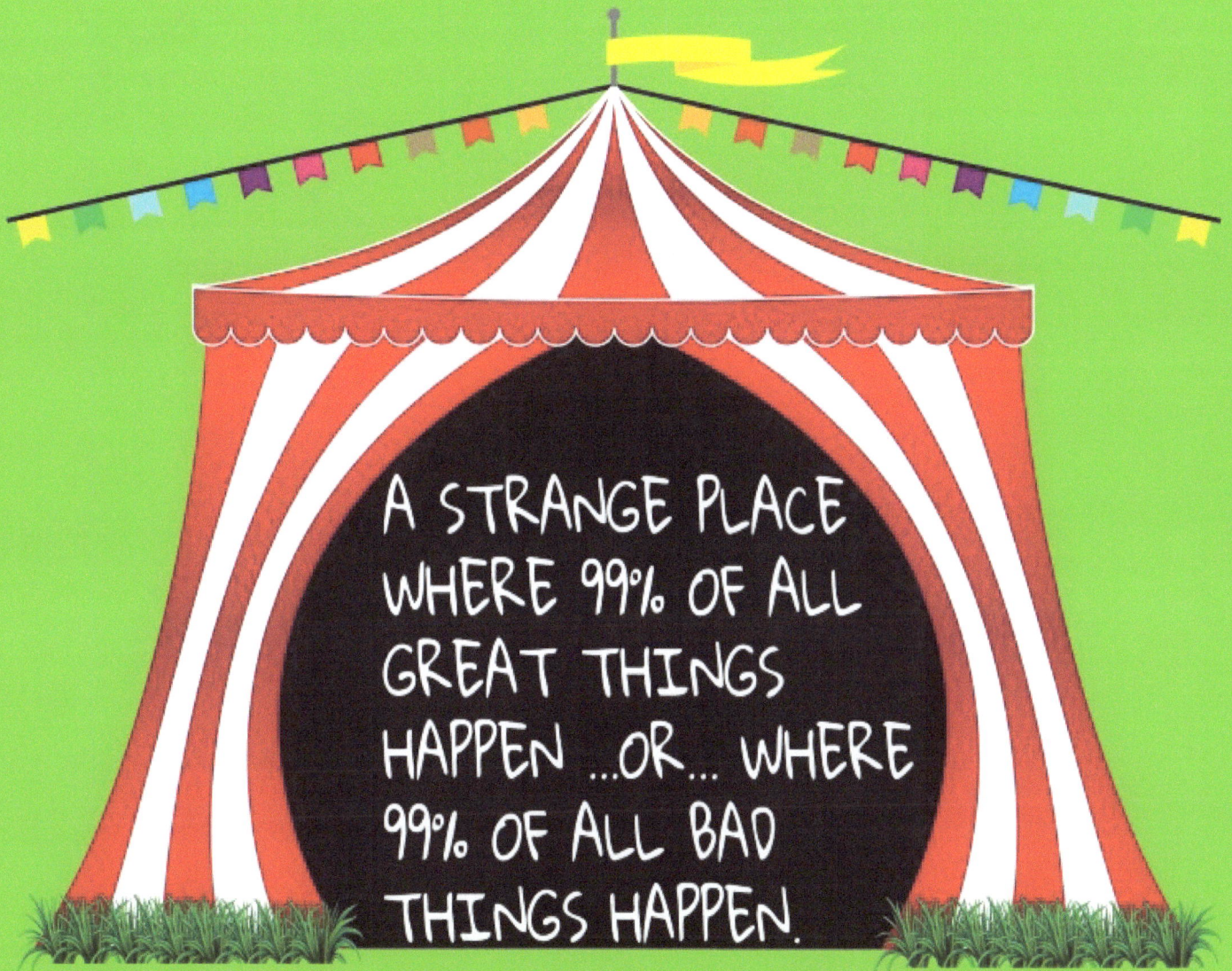

HARD TO BELIEVE THIS IS SO ???

When you make your choices in life...

Then you will know it is TRUE!

The Jury finds you guilty of saying horrible truths about some people's negative attitudes in Network Marketing.

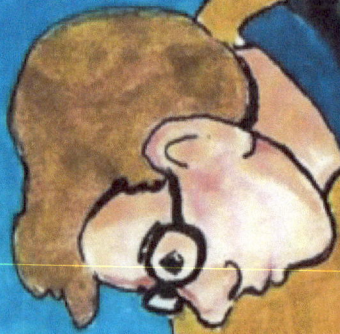

Good Fella, You're free to go.

Victoria Wundram

In N·W·M YOU DON'T HAVE TO KNOW MENTORS PERSONALLY TO GET GREAT!

MALE MENTORS

YOU

FEMALE MENTORS

HELP

25

C/S, ASK, WHAT CAN A SIDE HUSTLE DO FOR ME???

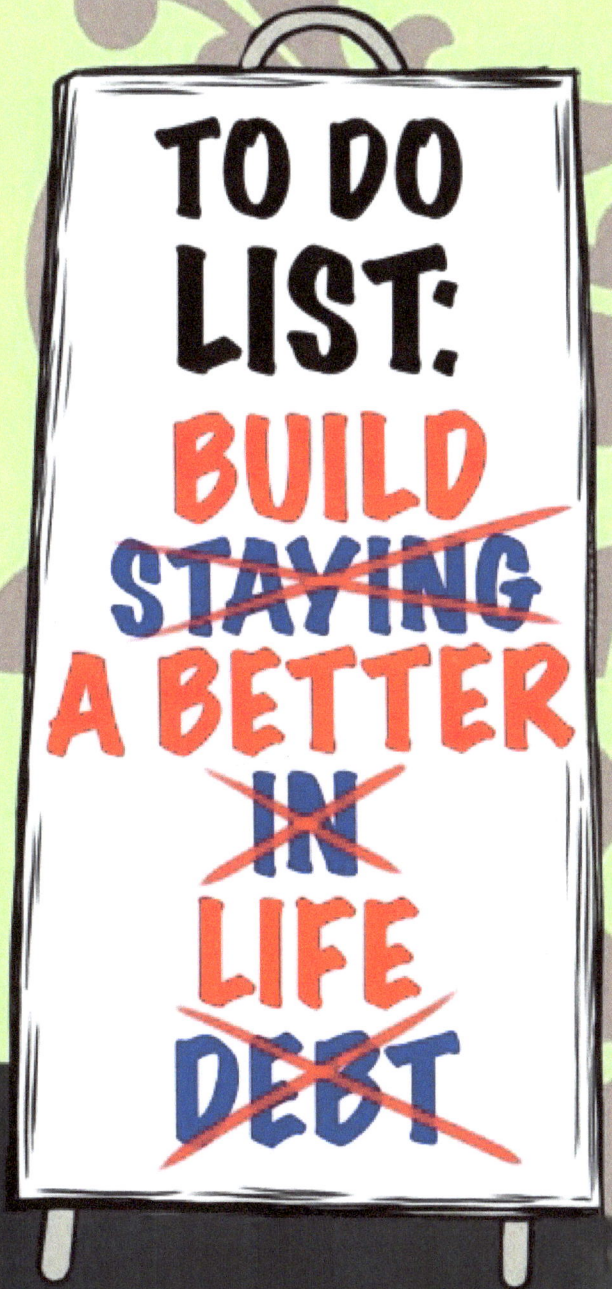

SAVINGS

TO DO LIST:
BUILD ~~STAYING~~
A BETTER ~~IN~~
LIFE ~~DEBT~~

C/S SAYS, IT'S A GOOD PRINCIPLE

"I DON'T NEED MY TEAM (GROUP OR DISTRIBUTION LINE) TO FOLLOW MY FOOTSTEPS, BUT, I NEED TO MAKE THEM WORTH FOLLOWING!!

JUST A PASSING THOUGHT

COMMON SENSE in N-W-M (or in life) does not mean "re-inventing the wheel" idea. It does mean traveling through life on 4 wheels, instead of 3. We can travel down any road we wish, with anyone we wish, and go the distant any time we chose.

AND IN THAT, that's where our problem lies-- in what we choose. You ever heard the term, 'stubborn as a mule'? If we were to apply COMMON SENSE to this story, what do you think it's talking about? As a person can be stubborn in all things that are both positive or negative. COMMON SENCE will be glad to leave it up to you, which direction you want to choose to travel.

ONE GOOD WAY you may want to travel is not by yourself. Now, when you choose to travel in your business life with others, you willing to learn. COMMON SENSE in N-W-M tells you to try and learn things most people will never learn.

    LEARN TO HAVE FUN
    LEARN TO LAUGH
    LEARN TO PLAY
    LEARN WHEN YOU WORK, NEVER PLAY
    LEARN TO HELP OTHERS
    LEARN TO TAKE HELP FROM OTHERS
    LEARN TO GROW BIGGER THAN YOU ARE NOW
    LEARN TO BE THANKFUL
    LEARN TO SHOW GRATITUDE
    AND , LEARN TO MAKE MONEY

    AND , PERHAPS, ETC. (i just love using that word)

ALMOST FORGOT to say, COMMON SENSE will tell you...
You cannot, or ever will, learn every thing in the business world. But, whatever you choose to do in the business world, you best LEARN everything.
KNOWLEDGE IS KING!!!

CIS ~~Says,~~ Knows,

Some **REWARDS**

mark the end of

GREAT

A ~~Good~~ Journey

in **N-W-M**

Some are just

the

BEGINNING

Some Philosophies in N-W-M

*Don't make Improvements, make Excuses

*Stop when it gets hard

*It's OK to cheat & lie if it benefits you

*Following your dreams is a waste of time

*Don't give people anything, just take

Something is wrong here,

BUT WHAT?

"I spent a lot of time worrying about my income potential. Then I got involved in **N-W-M**, created my own business, and then, *I built it & *I built it & *I built it. Now everything seems ok."

PAY-DAY TO PAY-DAY NATION

If anyone is looking for a good reason to research the field of Network Marketing, just read the 6 words above.

Business of every type will always try to produce a thing called Profit. Unfortunately, in many situations, the employees 'pay the price'.

Common Sense will try to inform you on what to look out for in the business world. Look...many things in the world are nasty, mean and brutal to everyone. It is YOU that always have to prepare for things that are nasty, mean and brutal in this world. Not your bosses, the employers, or even our government. Who is responsible for yourself and your family?---it is YOU!!!

Continued...

But, what can you do to change in a Pay-Day to Pay-Day Nation?

They say, money changes people for either the good or bad. Let's choose good. If you are employed, always try to do the best you can. Meanwhile, search other ways you can obtain more income. Make the discovery that will produce an extra source of income for you and your family. When looking for additional sources of income, there are "DO'S AND DON'T'S".

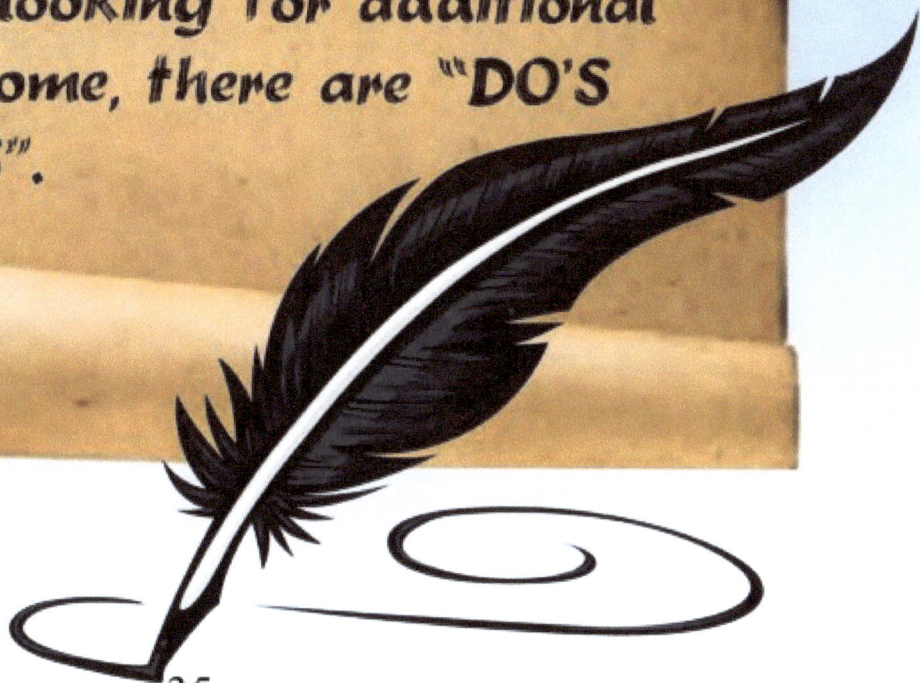

PAY=DAY TO PAY=DAY NATION

Concluded...

Let's start with the DONT'S:

Don't go after another (part-time) job. Here's why---

1. You will get low wages...small amount of money.
2. . Terrible working hours---time away from your family.
3. You will become good friends with the IRS...they get their money even before you see your paycheck.
4. There will never be extra rewards...no retirement funds, no vacation time, no health benefits.
5. Most likely, you will not learn new skills.
6. You put in your own negative results:

a)._____

b)._____

c)._____

Now, the DO'S:

1. Select Ownership.
2. Select new ways for improving your skills & Talents.
3. If you have ownership, you have Tax Deductions.
4. You have the opportunity to have things called profit, retirement funds, and a thing called--- GROWTH.

Well, I gave you 4 reasons for the DO'S and 6 reasons for the DONT'S. Friends, It's a numbers game. See my first book: COMMON SENSE - I THINK and study page 33.

If you think
Being in Network Markteing is

RISKY,

try working for someone else
for 40 years and living off
social security.

Warren Buffet
(sort of)

NWM IN A NUTSHELL!
If you want to go FAST GO ALONE

If you want to go FAR GO WITH Others

38

DIVERSIFY

TEAM BUILDING

SALES

MULTIPLE SOURCES OF IN COME

COMMUNICATION

OWNERSHIP

THEN YOU CAN SPIN A LOT OF DIFFERENT PLATES

40

41

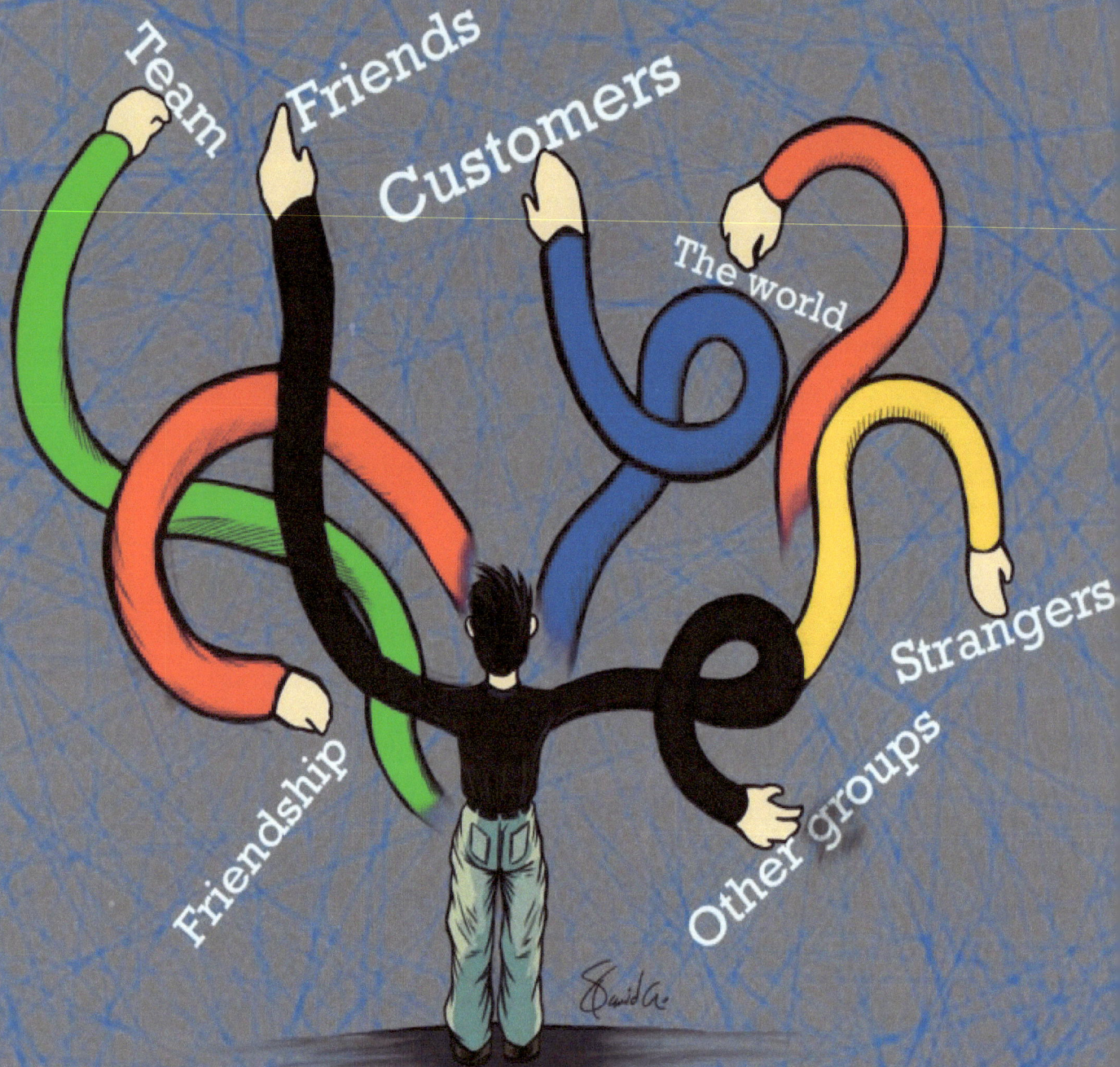

In NWM,
very few people will **EVER**
be accused of this. . .

Bibliobibuli

Definition: Those who read *too* much!

They are Both **RIGHT** one of them is **YOU**

Tell us All, Which **One**?

NEGATIVE

Positive

Network Marketing

To do better
in N·W·M
do this ↻

ACHIEVMENT
Plan 'A'
Plan 'B'
Plan 'C'
Plan 'D'
Plan 'E'

& ETC↰
(I JUST LOVE USING THAT WORD)

HEY!!
WHATEVER
IT TAKES

C/S knows in N-W-M,

2208 HOURS

MONTH 1
SUN MON TUE WEDS THUR FRI SAT
1 2 3 4 5
7 8 9 10 11
14 15 16 23

MONTH 2
SUN MON TUE WEDS THUR FRI SAT
6 1 2 3
4 5
11 12
18 19
25 26

MONTH 3
SUN MON TUE WEDS THUR FRI SAT
14
19 20 21 22 23 24 25
26 27 28 29 30

in a (any) NETWORK Business
it will most likely change your
LIFE (for the better)
FOREVER

Clue: Work Real Hard in N-W-M for 3 months and we will call that "just" a start

46

One of the many

SIMPLE TRUTHS

ABOUT

Network
Marketing

"The Secret to Getting Ahead is Getting STARTED."

Mark Twain

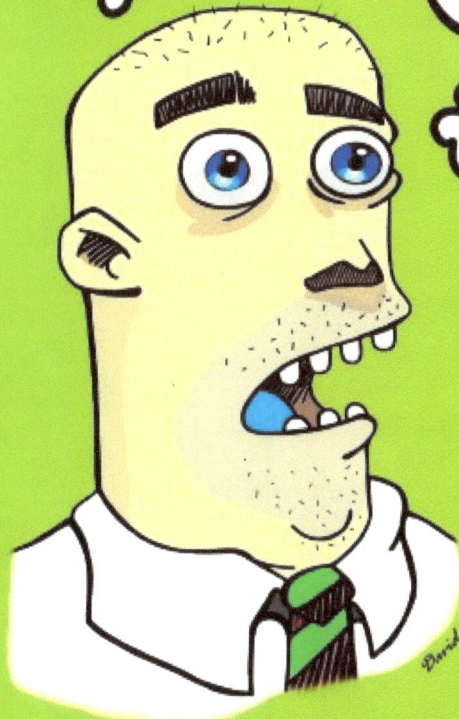

C/S WILL TELL YOU, IN IN N-W-M (AS WELL AS IN LIFE)

EVER SO OFTEN THIS IS BENEFICIAL TO MANY PEOPLE!

(MORE FORWARD IN LIFE, PLEASE)

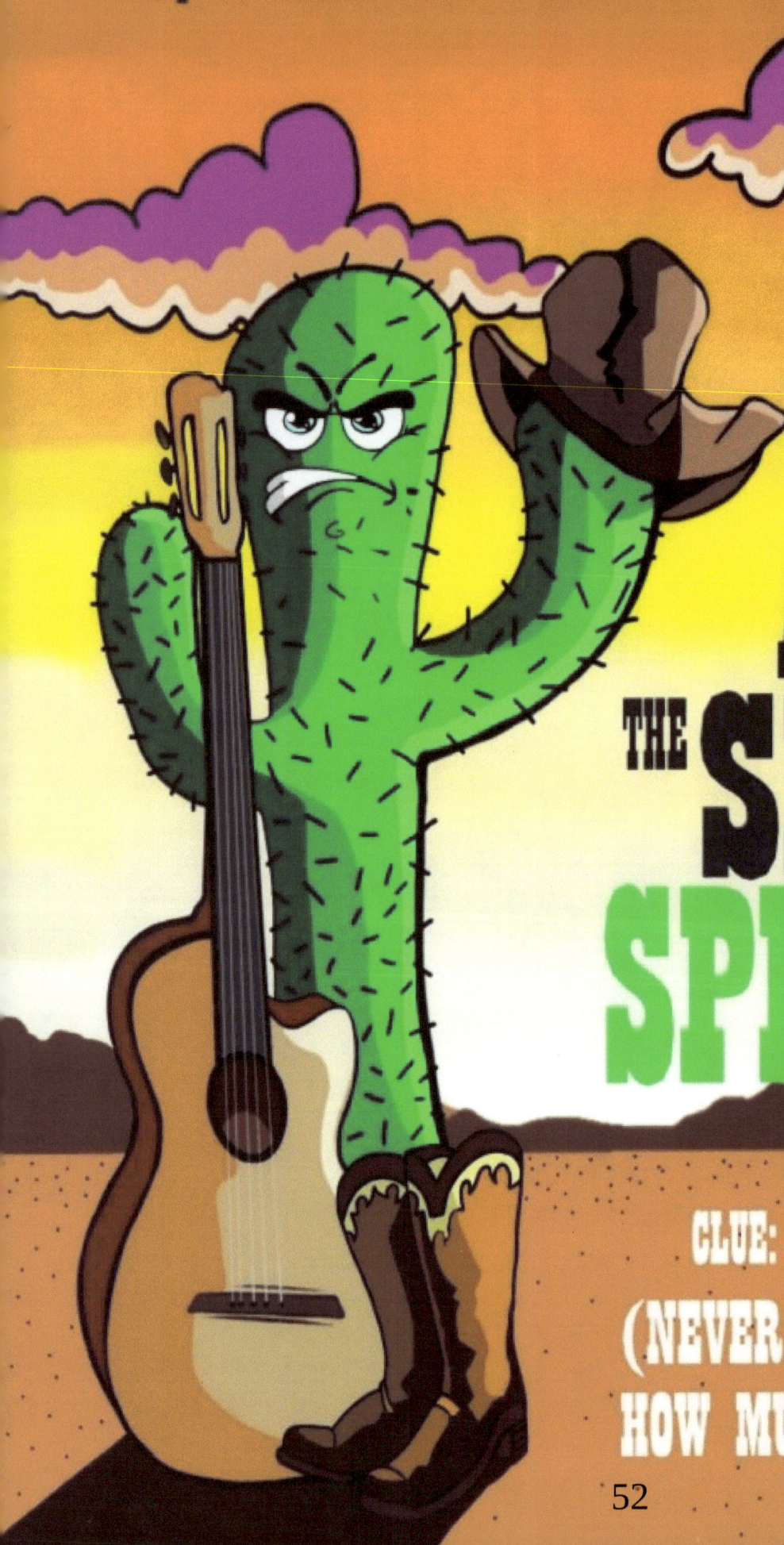

C/S HATES PEOPLE DOING THIS:

DON'T EVER ASK ANYONE THE SIZE OF THEIR SPREAD

CLUE: CARDINAL SIN (NEVER ASK A PERSON HOW MUCH THEY MAKE)

YOU CAN'T FOOL C/S IF YOU ARE A SMALL THINKER YOU'LL NEVER FIT INTO N·W·M

NETWORK MARKETING
THE GOOD LIFE

TEAM BUILDING IN A DIRECT MARKETING COMPANY

WHO'S HELPING WHO?
THEM-YOU-ME-OR-US?

CLUE: THE ANSWER IS EVERYBODY!!!

C/S - IN N.W.M, EVERYONE HAS ONE WHEN STARTING OUT

BLINDSPOT...

BLINDERS HELP WITH FOCUS, BUT NOT WITH LIMITS

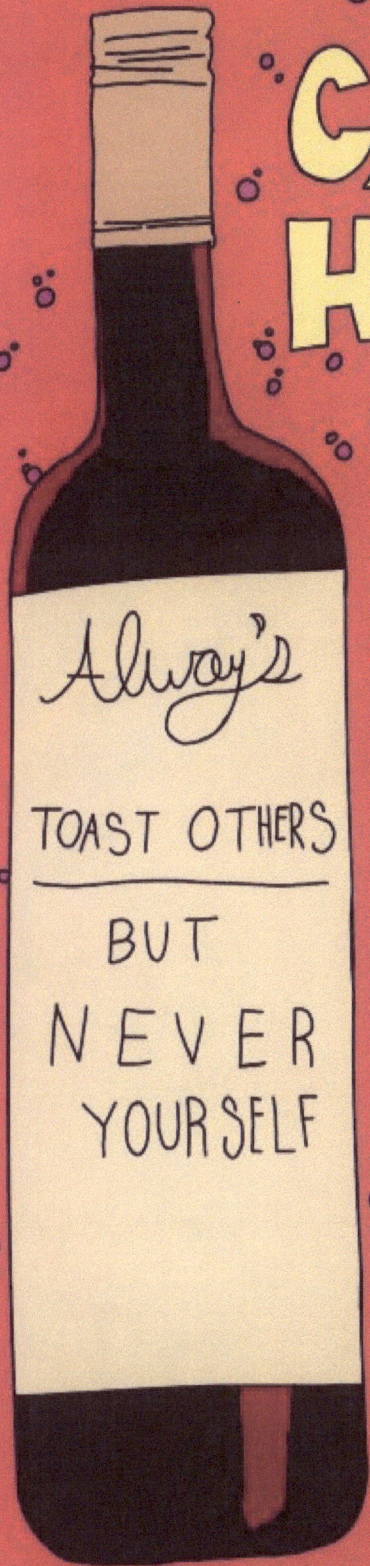

C/S HAS SEEN IT BEFORE.

WINE IN A BOTTLE ISN'T MADE FROM ONE GRAPE... WELL, A SUCCESSFUL LIFE ISN'T HAPPENING. FROM NWM ONE BOOK ONE EVENT ONE PERSON OR EVEN ONE YEAR!

Always TOAST OTHERS BUT NEVER YOURSELF

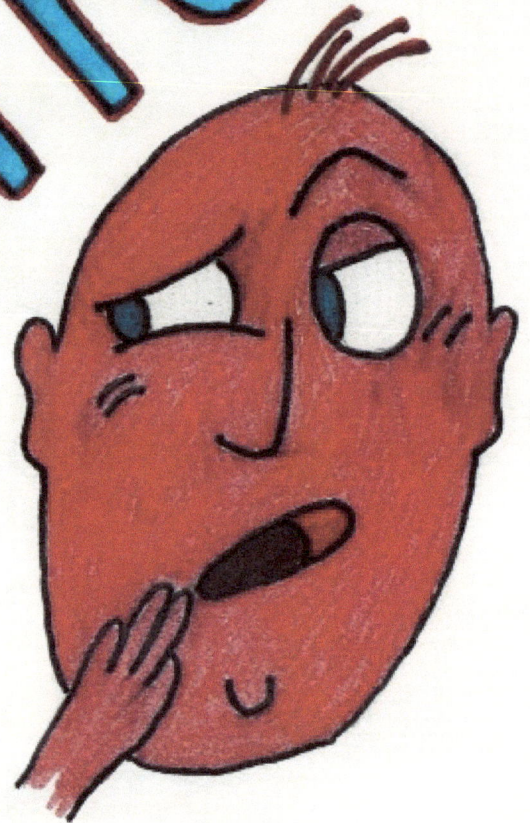

"IF I DO THINGS MY WAY IN N-W-M-W-M I WILL ALWAYS WIN"!

DOUBTFUL

C/S

Will ask you to understand that Word!!!

The End!

or...

Just the Beginning??

******SUMMARY******

ILLUSTRATORS CONTRIBUTION
(SUPER GROUP OF TALENT)

1). DESI GARCIA....................* FRONT PAGE
ALBUQUERQUE, NM   * Page 29.............."2 Years Old"
                         * Page 55.............."Blind spot".
                         * Page 56.............."What?".

2). Woody Woodrome..............* Page 1.............."Introduction #1".
ALBUQUERQUE, NM   * Page 2.............."Introduction #2".
                         * Page 3.............."Introduction #3".
                         * Page 4.............."Introduction #4".
                         * Page 5............"Introduction #5".
                         * Page 6............"Introduction #6".
                         * Page 11..........."Hello There".
                         * Page 12..........."Howdy".

3). Brenda Woodrome..............* Page 7.............."Rules".
ALBUQUERQUE, NM   * Page 8.............."Rules, cont.".
                         * Page 9.............."Rules, cont.".
                         * Page 10............"Rules, cont.".

4). Royeal Dee Jones..............* Page I.............."To Whom It May Concern".
VERNAL, UTAH   * Page II............."To Whom It May Concern, cont.".
                         * Page III............"To Whom It May Concern, cont.".

5). Ethan Wenberg..................* Page 48............"Urgency/Emergency".
CHAPEL HILL, NC

6). Bob Anderson......................* Page 19............"Shrinking Leisure Time".
ALBUQUERQUE, NM   * Page 20............"Shrinking Leisure Time, cont.".
                         * Page 30............"Just a Passing Thought.".
                         * Page 31............"Rewards".
                         * Page 32............"Philosophies".
                         * Page 33............"Income Potential".
                         * Page 34............"Pay-Day To Pay-Day Nation".
                         * Page 35............"Pay-Day To Pay-Day Nation, cont.".
                         * Page 36............"Pay-Day To Pay-Day Nation, cont.".

7).   Sarah Anderson....................* Page 59............"The End".
       ALBUQUERQUE, NM

8).   Tyler Overall.......................* Page 25............"Mentors".
       ALBUQUERQUE, NM   * Page 57............"One Grape"

9).   Bill Dulsky...........................* Page 45............"Whatever It Takes".
       RIO RANCHO, NM   * Page 53.............."Can't Fool".
                                * Page 58.............."Doubtful".

10).   Felisha Lapchyrski................* Page 22............"Stop".
       MAUI, HAWAII

11).   David Alvarado.....................* Page 13............"Into The Sunset".
       MEXICO   * Page 14............."Win".
                                * Page 27............."Hustle"
                                * Page 28............."Footsteps"
                                * Page 39............."Diversity"
                                * Page 40............."Trainee Wanted".
                                * Page 41............."Horses".
                                * Page 42............."Reach Out".
                                * Page 49............."Lopsided".
                                * Page 50............."Kick".
                                * Page 51............."Head In The Clouds".
                                * Page 52............."Spread".
                                * Page 54............."Team Building".

12).   Victoria Wundram................* Page 24............"Jury".
       MAUI, HAWAII

13).   Maureen 'Moe' Rouch..........* Page 15....................."Residual".
       RIO RANCHO, NM   * Page 16...................."Network Marketing".
                                * Page 17...................."Football".
                                * Page 18...................."Surf".
                                * Page 21...................."Relationship".
                                * Page 23...................."Tomorrow".
                                * Page 26...................."No".
                                * Page 37...................."Risky".
                                * Page 44...................."Both Right".
                                * Page 46...................."2208 Hours".
                                * Page 47...................."Simple Truth".

14). Nicole Anderson.................* Page 38............."Jury".
    RIO RANCHO, NM   * Page 43............."Bibliobibuti".
                           * Page 59............."Hee-Haw".

15). Peter Menice.....................* Cartoon—Self Portrait
    CORRALES, NM

MY THOUGHTS......................

NETWORK MARKETING AND COMMON SENSE TOGETHER... MERCY, WHAT WILL I THINK OF NEXT.

I HAVE COME TO REALIZE NETWORK MARKETING HAS BEEN AROUND FOR A LONG TIME. LITTLE HAS CHANGED. THERE IS A COMPANY (CORPORATION), PRODUCTS OR SERVICES, WORKING SYSTEMS, PAY PLANS AND SOME TYPE OF DISTRIBUTION PROGRAM. THE BIGGEST THING THAT ALWAYS CHANGES IS PEOPLE. AND TWO THINGS WILL HAPPEN--- SUCCESS OR FAILURE. IN MY BUSINESS CAREERS, I SEEN IT HAPPEN MANY, MANY TIMES IN MANY WAYS.

THE BEAUTY ABOUT IT IS SIMPLE. COMMON SENSE SHOULD BE USED IN MAKING A LIFE IN THE NETWORK MARKETING INDUSTRY. SEE, NETWORK MARKETING WILL NEVER CHANGE. SO WHAT HAS TO CHANGE? I THINK YOU KNOW THE ANSWER ALREADY. Most people don't do well in network marketing because they don't improve the most important thing---themselves.

I DO NOT BELIEVE FOR A MOMENT, I HAVE ALL THE RIGHT ANSWERS YOU NEED. BUT, I HOPE MY BOOK GIVES YOU A GOOD BEGINNING.

THANKS A LOT,

Tom Burns

Tom Burns
burnstom@comcast.net
www.commonsense-ithink.com

65

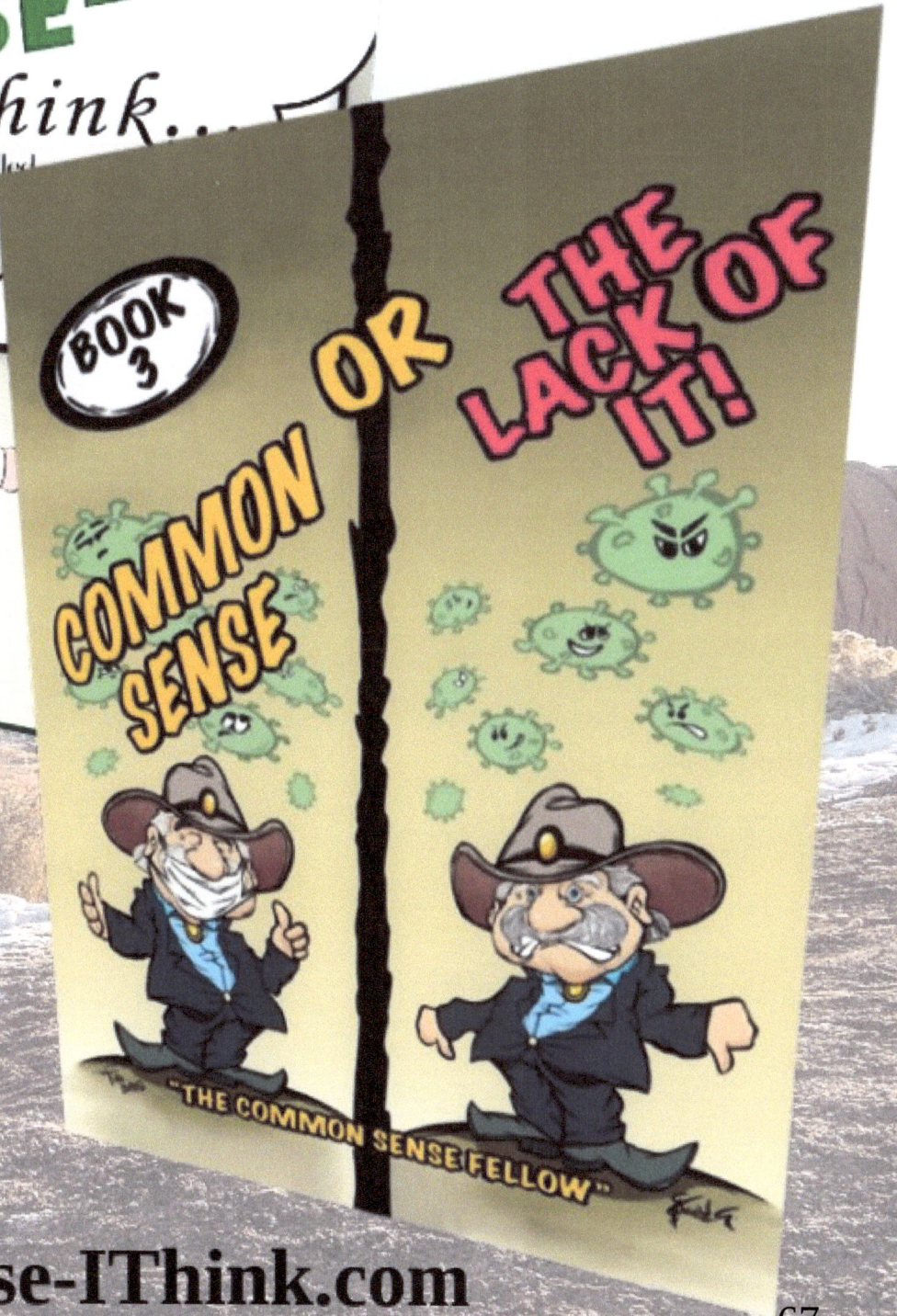

CommonSense-IThink.com

www.ingramcontent.com/pod-product-compliance
Lightning Source LLC
Chambersburg PA
CBHW052047190326
41521CB00002BA/139